FABULOUS PUGS

FABULOUS PUGS

FEATURING *Charlie Knapp*

BY *Lisa Knapp*

PHOTOGRAPHS BY *Danny Strickland*

STEWART, TABORI & CHANG
NEW YORK

Published in 2006 by Stewart, Tabori & Chang
An imprint of Harry N. Abrams, Inc.

ISBN-13: 978-1-58479-531-5
ISBN-10: 1-58479-531-X

Designers: Lisa Knapp and Kay Deimling
Cover Design: Galen Smith
Production Manager: Kim Tyner

The text of this book was composed in Times New Roman, Copperplate Gothic, and Refreshment Stand.

Printed and bound in China
10 9 8 7 6 5 4 3 2 1

harry n. abrams, inc.

a subsidiary of La Martinière Groupe

115 West 18th Street
New York, NY 10011
www.hnabooks.com

Dedicated to my always loving husband, *Steve*.

Foreword

After a year of scouring every dog book, dog magazine, and dog website, I finally decided that a pug was the ideal dog for me. Despite my husband's hesitation that a dog—any dog—would be a good addition to our household, I persevered and found the perfect breeder in Tennessee.

I went a little overboard in my preparation for The Arrival, acquiring a large collection of toys and treats. The consequences of not having children! When we made the trek to pick up the pug, the breeder announced, "She's a little wild." Wide-eyed, we watched her race around the kennel at full speed, performing less-than-perfect figure-eights that segued into side-to-side maneuvers like a crazed Alpine skier. I realized, with budding pride, the tiny creature's willfulness as she worked ferociously to decapitate what had been an adorable stuffed bunny.

We named her Charlie. Back home in Atlanta, as the cooler autumn weather arrived, we kept our beloved spring-born pup warm as we progressed from T-shirts to sweaters and, finally, to coats. Coats presented a serious challenge, for pugs are curvaceous, with a rather short back, and with a head that rests on what can only be described as the absence of a neck.

But thanks to my love of sewing, and after many failed prototypes, Charlie was soon previewing a fabulous new coat on the runways of our Atlanta neighborhood. Pug haute couture became Charlie's and my new obsession. Invitations to the most sought-after soirées began filling our mailbox, and this proud mother was happy to design and manufacture pug fashions for puppy fêtes of all persuasions.

And then it hit me: why not share my Charlie with the world? That's when the literary journey began that led to *Fabulous Pugs*. The combination of my sewing skills and Charlie's modeling abilities has resulted in this walk through pug history and pop culture, not to mention a feast for the pug fashion connoisseur.

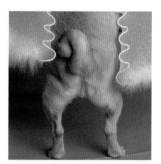

Each costume—tiny hats, dresses, and coats—was born of extensive research and tireless effort behind the sewing machine. When the time finally came for the photo shoot, Charlie sat patiently, finding her muse for characters ranging from Henry VIII to Notorious P.U.G. A consummate professional, Charlie never complained, hid in her trailer, or asked for her union rep—she was a real trooper.

I hope you enjoy this fabulous pug's journey through history!

Acknowledgments

I would like to thank the exceptionally talented Danny Strickland of Zoom Design for his wonderful photography; Kay Deimling, who has the patience of a saint, for her wonderful art direction; my mother Elizabeth Herndon, sister Stella Herndon, and brother Ashley Herndon, all of whom buoyed my sometimes sagging enthusiasm; and, most important, my husband, for always encouraging me to express my creativity on many different levels.

Eve Pug

"Aaahhh, temptation, temptation, temptation!"

Cave Woman Pug

Cro-Magnon Pug, early Pugo sapiens

Confuciuspug

Philosopher Pug

Confucius says: a wise Pug's bark is always bigger than his bite

Julius Pugustus Caesar

"Et tu, Poodle?"

Attila the Pug

Pug of the Huns

Leif Ericpug

Viking Pug

Lady Godivapug

Naked pug in Coventry Market

Genghis Pug

The Mongol Pug

William Tellpug

Legendary Swiss pug

Count Pugula

Transylvanian Pug of Darkness

Queen Isabellapug

The Catholic Pug

Henry VIII Pug

"He was a pug of an unbounded stomach."

Shakespeare**pug**

"To eat or not to eat, that is the question."

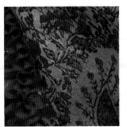

Pugahontas

Native American pug

 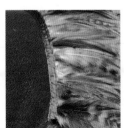 

Louis XIV Pug

The Sun Pug

Marie Antoinette*pug*

"Vive la Pug!"

Napoleon Bonapug

Defeated at the Battle of Pugaloo

Queen Victoriapug

Longest-reigning pug queen

Jesse Jamespug

Desperado pug

Pancho Villapug

Revolutionary Mexican pug

Lawrence of Pugrabia

"All pugs dream, but not equally."

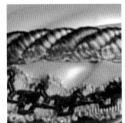

Mao Tse-pug

Founder of the Pugs' Republic of China

Sitting Bullpug

Sioux pug

Puglett O'Hara

"As God is my witness, I'll never be hungry again"...maybe?

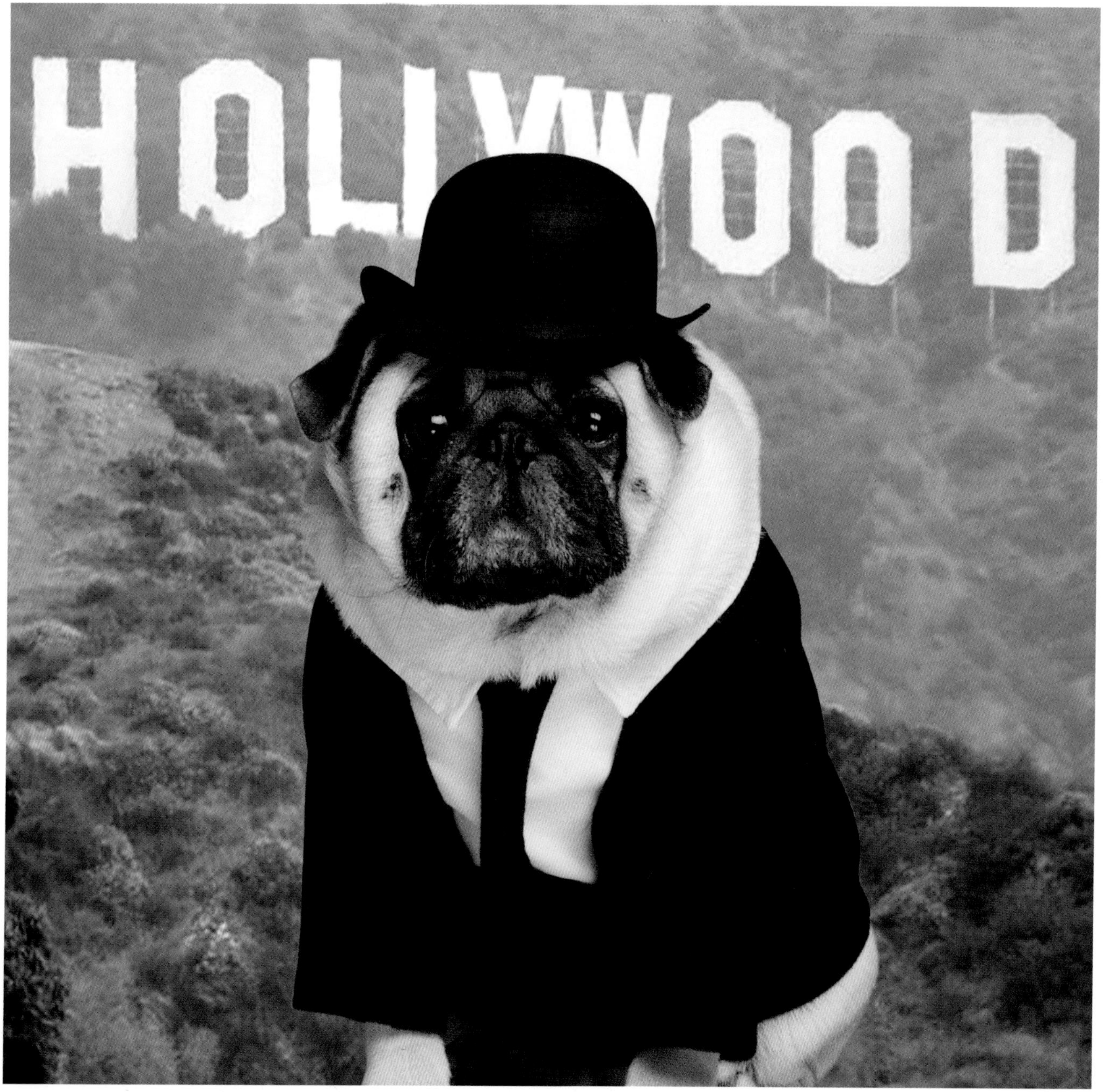
HOLLYWOOD

Charlie Chaplinpug

The Pug Tramp

Glinda the Good Pug

"Are you a good pug, or a bad pug?"

Carmen Mirandapug

Brazilian samba pug

June Cleaverpug

The pug who vacuums in heels and pearls

Liz Taylorpug

Pug on a Hot Tin Roof

Kirk Pugless

"I am Spartapug!"

Pug Hefner

Publisher of Playpug magazine

Marilyn Pugroe

Norma Jean Pug

Jackie Pug 1961

Jackie Pug

The perfect head for a pillbox hat

First Pug on the Moon

"The pug has landed."

Spockpug

"...to boldly go where no pug has gone before!"

Andy Warholpug

World-famous pug...for fifteen minutes

PLAYPUG

HERE'S CHARLIE

EXCLUSIVE

Photos Of Charlie Taking A Bath

ALL NEW ALL NUDE

High School Video Tape Shows Her Rubber Toys

INTERVIEW

Local Cat Tells All

Playpug

*Likes: trips to the park, crumbs off the
floor, and long naps on the sofa*

Madonnapug

The Material Pug

Notorious P.U.G.

The gansta pug

Angel Pug

"Heaven must be missing an angel pug."